Gym Rats

True Stories About Punching, Pedaling, and Powerlifting

Michael Dahlie

SCHOLASTIC INC.

**New York Toronto London Auckland Sydney
Mexico City New Delhi Hong Kong Buenos Aires**

**Cover photograph
Michael Aron**

**Illustrations
Kevin Rechin**

Copyright © 2002 by Scholastic Inc.
All rights reserved. Published by Scholastic Inc.
Printed in the U.S.A.

ISBN 0-439-12335-6
(meets NASTA specifications)

SCHOLASTIC, READ 180, and associated logos and designs are trademarks and/or registered trademarks of Scholastic Inc.
LEXILE is a trademark of MetaMetrics, Inc.

6   7   8   9   10   23   10   09   08   07   06

Contents

Introduction

Do you like working out? Get a kick out of sweating? Just like hanging around the gym? If you answered "yes" to any of these questions, chances are you're a "gym rat." But don't get upset. That's just a name for people who love to exercise.

If you're a gym rat, you're in good company. Some of the nation's top athletes are gym rats at heart. They can't get enough of pumping weights, riding a **stationary** bike, or attacking that climbing wall.

In this book, you'll meet five gym rats. These men and women spend a lot of time working out. And they all have something to show for it. They are excellent athletes. And they've developed skills that have helped them in other areas of their lives.

Spin Doctor: Erin Elberson

In just one workout, Erin Elberson travels all over the world. She rides her bike through deserts, over mountains, and along oceans.

At the end of her workout, Erin's right back where she started. In fact, she never even leaves the gym. Erin is a spinner. She uses her imagination and a stationary bike to go to far-off lands.

What exactly is spinning?

Spinning is like taking a long bike trip without ever leaving the gym. In a spinning class, everyone rides special stationary bikes. The bikes have a **"resistance** knob," which makes it harder or easier to ride.

During the class, the teacher talks to you. She helps you imagine your trip. She tells you to imagine that you're going up steep roads, down hills, or along flat land. For instance, she

Erin Elberson is a spinning instructor. She says spinning has taught her how to concentrate and work hard. "I love the mental part of spinning more than anything else."

might say, "We're riding down a steep hill, and in the distance we can see the ocean."

As the teacher talks, you adjust your resistance knob to match the kind of land she's describing. And you listen to her to help picture your trip. It's great.

How did you get started?

I started spinning in 1996. I decided to go to a spinning class at my gym. At first, I did it once or twice a week. It was part of my regular workout. But soon I got hooked and did it every day.

I loved the mental part of spinning more than anything else. I was fresh out of college. I needed to get in shape. And I wanted to develop more confidence.

One thing led to another. Before long, I was training to be a spinning teacher. Now I train other teachers.

Describe a typical week.

I teach two or three classes per week. I also ride in classes taught by other people. And I do two to three hours of weight training. All that's on top of working 40 hours a week as a **physical therapist**. I'm pretty busy. But I love it.

Do you have a special diet?

I eat healthy foods. I make sure I don't eat too much fat. And I try to eat lots of fruits and vegetables. But I also love chocolate. I never apologize for eating it!

What benefits do you get from spinning?

Spinning works out your body and your mind. It improves concentration and exercises your heart and lungs. It also gives you confidence. Many times, the route that your teacher describes can be a symbol for something in your life. For instance, a mountain might stand for a goal. Getting over the mountain will give you confidence to achieve that goal.

What's your favorite thing about spinning?

I like working out with other people. Energy is **contagious**! I'm inspired by the people I spin with. We all do our own thing. We all work toward our own goals. But we do it together.

What's your gym like?

I've got a great gym! The best thing is that it's calm and really personal. There are a lot of beginners there. So, most people help each other out. There aren't many show-offs, and people don't compete with one another.

Has spinning helped you in other areas of your life?

Yes. Right now, I'm learning how to kayak. Kayaks are special canoes made for fast rivers. Spinning has taught me how to concentrate and work hard. That makes learning new things much easier. Knowing how to set a goal and achieve it is what spinning is all about.

What has Erin learned from spinning? How does that affect her life?

Quench That Thirst!

Your body needs water for almost everything it does. Water carries vitamins and other **nutrients**. It helps your joints move smoothly. It protects you from getting hurt. And it keeps your body cool.

Here are some important tips to remember.

- Drink eight glasses of water every day. During hot days or hard workouts, drink more.

- Stay away from coffee, tea, and soda. They have **caffeine**, which takes water out of your body.

- Drink 16 to 20 ounces of water two hours before a workout. That's about two glasses.

- Keep a water bottle with you at the gym. Drink water every 5 to 10 minutes during a workout.

Captain Curl: Lou Cortezzo

Everyone knows what weightlifting is. But have you heard of powerlifting? In this sport, athletes use their strength to lift super-heavy weights.

*Lou Cortezzo holds many world powerlifting records. And he's only 22 years old! In fact, his arms are so strong that he's known as "Captain Curl." He can lift his own weight and then some. And his **biceps** are 19 inches around.*

How did you get into powerlifting?

Some people at my gym said I should compete. I started learning about it on the Internet and found out about a meet. I entered it and did really well.

I was especially good at the curling competitions. Curling tests the strength of your arm muscles. After that meet, I entered more. It all took off from there.

Lou Cortezzo is a world champion powerlifter. Powerlifters are *true* athletes, Lou says. "We don't get rich or famous. We compete for ourselves."

What's your typical workout routine?

I try to do some **aerobic exercise** every day. That's training that works out your heart and lungs. Powerlifting keeps your muscles strong. But to be really healthy, you have to exercise your lungs and heart, too.

Okay, back to the routine. On Monday, I work out my chest, arms, and shoulders.

On Tuesday, I work out my legs.

On Wednesday, I focus on my back and biceps.

On Thursday, I do lots of aerobic training. I run or ride a bike.

On Friday, I work out my chest, arms, and shoulders again.

On Saturday, I work out my back and biceps.

And Sunday, I usually take off. I have to rest sometime!

Do you eat anything special?

I try to stay away from fast food. I also try not to eat **saturated fats**. Of course, sometimes I cheat and eat a burger. Sometimes you *gotta!*

What's the powerlifting scene like?

It's a lot of work. But it's also a lot of fun. I see many of the same people at each competition. And I always meet new people. I met many of my best friends powerlifting. It's even how I met my future wife!

Which athletes do you respect the most?

I respect all athletes who push themselves to the limit. I have always liked powerlifting because the athletes are *true* athletes. They work hard for their success. But they don't get rich or famous like people in other sports. We compete for ourselves.

What do you do when you're not at the gym, working out?

I work in an office. I market products. That means I try to spread the word about things people might want or need. In a way, its like what I do with powerlifting. I'm always trying to **promote** my sport!

How do you promote powerlifting?

I plan meets. I judge them. I send out flyers. I get other people to compete. And I try to get

Don't try this at home! If you're interested in powerlifting, Lou says, start slow. It takes a lot of training to lift this kind of weight without injuring yourself.

kids to come watch. When I was young, I didn't know about powerlifting. So I work hard to make sure young kids know about it.

When should kids start lifting?

It's always good for kids to work out. But they shouldn't push themselves too hard. I don't think kids under the age of 16 should compete. But everyone is different. Some people grow faster than others. If you want to start a new exercise program, talk to your doctor first!

Why do you think Lou likes powerlifting so much?

Building Biceps

Want to build your biceps? Talk to the expert!

Lou "Captain Curl" Cortezzo has set world records with his. He competes in the "strict curl." In this event, you lift weight from your thighs to your chest, using only your arm muscles.

How much can Lou curl? If he follows the rules, he can lift 210 pounds!

Here are some tips from the master himself.

Lift Safe

Always know your limits, especially if you're a beginner. It's easy to get hurt if you do too much too fast.

Also, talk to your doctor before starting a new exercise program. He or she will know what your body can handle.

Set Realistic Goals

Don't be fooled by the biceps you see in comic books. Say these superheroes were real. Some would have arms 30 inches around!

Compare that to Lou's arms. They're some of the strongest in the world. But they're 19 inches around.

Find a Good Gym

Working out at a gym can really help. Having

other people around will make you work harder. Lifting with a partner will also make your workout a lot safer.

Exercises

There are no magic exercises. It just takes a lot of hard work. Here's what Captain Curl does to build up his biceps.

- 3 to 4 sets of standing curls with a barbell. (A barbell is the long bar you hold with both hands.)

- 2 to 3 sets of seated curls with dumbbells. (Dumbbells are the smaller weights you hold in each hand.)

- 1 set of "21s." That's 7 curls from hip to chest, 7 curls from chest to shoulder, and 7 full-range curls from thigh to shoulder.

But don't just try these exercises on your own! Get advice from an expert first. A coach or P.E. teacher would be a good place to start.

Ski Queen: Sarah Billmeier

At the age of five, Sarah Billmeier lost her leg to cancer. But nine years later, she was one of the best disabled skiers in the U.S.

How did she do it? Well, talent played a big part. But it also took lots of hours in the gym.

Was it worth it? Sarah thinks so. All that training led to gold medals at the Paralympics. That's the Olympics for people with disabilities.

Sarah's hard work also taught her discipline. And that's helped her achieve goals in other areas of her life.

How did you get into skiing?

I started skiing when I was eight. I joined a program that taught people with disabilities how to ski. They taught me to ski on one ski. I used poles that have ski tips on the ends.

It was hard at first. But I loved it! After a

Sarah Billmeier is a world-class disabled skier. Downhill races are her favorite. "You can go as fast as you want," she says. For Sarah, that means speeds of over 60 miles per hour!

Left: **Sarah, off the slopes.**

couple of years, I started racing. I've been competing ever since.

Tell us about the different ski races.

There's the downhill. That tests how fast you can go. Then there are three **slalom** events. In slalom races, you ski around markers—called gates—as you go down the hill.

What's your favorite event?

The downhill is my favorite. You go really fast. Sometimes you're skiing more than 60 miles per hour!

They put up fences along the edge of the course. So if you lose control, you won't go flying off the mountain. You can go as fast as you want.

What's it like to compete at top levels?

I've been in three Paralympics so far. I went to my first when I was 14. I had no idea what I was getting into. But I loved it.

The best part is meeting other skiers. The worst part is that it can be stressful. There are huge crowds and lots of reporters. Sometimes it's hard to deal with all that. But it's worth it.

Where was your favorite place to travel?

Probably Japan. The Paralympics were there in 1998. All our events were sold out. And the fans were great. It was really special.

What are you most proud of?

I didn't quit after a serious injury.

It happened just before the 1994 games. I

hurt the end of my missing leg. I fell and broke the remaining part of my thigh bone.

I did it while skiing. So I had to deal with lots of mental issues. I lost a lot of confidence in my abilities, especially in the downhill. And that has always been my best event.

But I came back in five weeks. And I did well in my events. So I was happy about that.

Injuries are always more mental than physical. I was proud that I could deal with my fear.

Are you ever self-conscious because of your missing leg?

Not really. I have met many older skiers with disabilities. I really like and respect them. They have made me feel comfortable. And they have given me confidence. So I don't really worry about what other people think.

How do you train?

In the winter, I ski from eight in the morning till one or two in the afternoon. After that, I go home for a couple of hours.

Then I head to the gym for an hour or two.

I ride a stationary bike to warm up. Then I either do more aerobic training or lift weights.

I try to stick to this schedule. But sometimes it's tough when I'm traveling for competitions. I just do the best I can.

Why do you spend time at the gym?

Well, say you're a ski racer and you don't go to the gym. You'll probably lose your race. Strength is a big part of skiing. You have to work out if you want to compete.

How did you work out while your leg was broken?

It was crazy. I was in a cast from my chest to my thigh. I'd ride the stationary bike with this big cast on. The problem was that the cast was so hot! But the bike was the best way to keep in shape. So I had to do it.

How has skiing helped you in the rest of your life?

I think training for a sport teaches you a lot. You learn how to work hard. And you learn how to deal with pressure. It also gives you confidence. It helps you to believe in yourself.

What are your goals for the future?

Right now, I'm getting ready for the next Paralympics. They're in Salt Lake City. I'd love to do well there. It would be great to win at home in the U.S.

How has Sarah overcome hurdles in her life?

How Are You Eating?

You've heard it before. You are what you eat. So, are you a health nut? Or are you a junk-food junky? Take this quiz and find out.

1. How often do you drink water?

   a. Water? Who drinks water?

   b. I stop by the water fountain between classes.

   c. I drink about eight glasses a day.

2. How many meals do you eat each day?

   a. My day is one long meal.

   b. Three. I eat breakfast, lunch, and dinner. I also have an afternoon snack.

   c. I eat one meal a day.

3. Do you eat breakfast?

   a. Every morning!

   b. Never! Sleep is more important to me!

   c. Sometimes I grab a doughnut.

4. How many fruits and vegetables do you eat in a day?

   a. Does strawberry ice cream count? I eat that once a day.

   b. I eat a piece of fruit every day. But I never eat vegetables.

   c. You're not going to believe this. But I love fruits and vegetables. I eat them every day!

5. How often do you drink milk? Or eat cheese or yogurt?

   a. I never drink milk. But sometimes I eat cheese doodles.

   b. Maybe once a day.

   c. Three times a day.

How'd You Do?
Add up your score using the key below.

Question 1:   a = 0   b = 5   c = 10

   Did you know that most of your body is water? Well, it is. Blood is 83% water. Bones are 22% water. And muscle is 75% water. So drink up! You'll feel better.

Question 2:   a = 5   b = 10   c = 0

   Food is the body's fuel. If you don't eat, your body won't work for you. So be sure to eat breakfast, lunch, and dinner. And forget those candy bars. If you want a snack, grab a piece of fruit. Or have some cheese and crackers.

Question 3:   a = 10   b = 0   c = 1

Why is breakfast so important? You need to re-fuel after sleeping all night. If you skip breakfast, you'll probably eat more later in the day.

So make your breakfast a good one. Try for a mix of **carbohydrates** and protein. Cereal with low-fat milk and a banana is a good breakfast. So is whole wheat toast with peanut butter and apple slices. And remember one thing. A doughnut is not a healthy breakfast!

Question 4:   a = 0   b = 5   c = 10

Your body is a complex machine. It needs many different nutrients. So eat different fruits and vegetables every day. That way, you'll get more of the vitamins and minerals you need.

Question 5:   a = 0   b = 5   c = 10

Milk, cheese, and yogurt are dairy products. And dairy products are full of calcium. That's good news for your bones. They need calcium to stay healthy and strong. If you treat your bones well, they won't let you down!

The Final Result

45–50 Health Nut

You're right on track! Keep doing what you're doing. Make sure you eat lots of whole grains. And have some protein every day.

25–40 Sometime Slacker

Hmmm. You're doing some things right. But you need to improve in other areas. Look at your answers. On which ones did you score 0 or 5 points? How could you improve your score? Should you drink more water? How about eating breakfast?

0–20 Junk-Food Junky

There's good news. With a few changes, you can be healthier. But there's bad news, too. If you don't make some changes soon, you'll be sorry! You'll feel tired all the time. Your hair and eyes will look dull. You might even get sick. So, get healthy now!

0–50 Yeah, You!

Think before you eat. Say you're hungry. Don't just grab whatever you see. Try to eat different kinds of foods every day. Eat grains, fruits and vegetables, dairy products, and protein. Drink plenty of water. And go easy on the sweets! It might be tough at first. But it's worth it!

Motivation Man: Kirk Miller

Like hanging around with other gym rats? Try getting a job like Kirk Miller's. He's a personal trainer. And he actually gets paid to spend time at the gym!

Of course, he has a lot of responsibility. People hire him to whip them into shape. Sometimes that can be hard work. But Kirk loves it! He says he can make anyone physically fit.

What is a personal trainer?

A personal trainer is like a personal coach. It's my job to make sure my **clients** work hard. And I make sure they do their exercises correctly.

Sometimes I'm a teacher. But mostly I'm there to push people to do their best. I guess you could call me a professional **motivator.**

© James Levin

Personal trainer Kirk Miller calls himself a "professional motivator." It's his job to help gym rats get the most out of their workouts. Here, he helps a client warm up.

Who uses personal trainers?

All sorts of people. I've worked with kids, teenagers, and adults. Mostly I train people who just want to get in shape. But I also help people train for specific sports.

How did you get into this?

I grew up in England. I learned to play rugby there. That's a sport sort of like football. Speed is important in the game.

I wanted to get faster. One of my teachers was a weightlifter. He said lifting weights would make me quicker. And he was right. After that, I wanted to learn more about training.

When did you start working as a trainer?

I got my first job when I was in college. I went to a school in New York City. I worked at a gym nearby. I spent a lot of time working out. And soon I started training people.

These days, I'm just a part-time trainer. I have another job working at a business. But I love training people. So I kept a few clients. I train people about ten hours a week.

What do you like best about being a personal trainer?

I've made some great friendships. When I train someone, I also become their personal listener. So I really get to know my clients. I really care about them. And I want them to get healthy and strong.

What's a typical day for you?

I get up at 4:45 A.M. I take the subway to the gym. My first client gets there at 6:00 A.M. After that, I work with two more people. That's one client an hour for three hours.

At 9:00 A.M., I train myself for half an hour. But I also work in an office during the day. So after training myself, I go to work.

After work, I go back to the gym. After my second workout, I have rugby practice from 7:30 to 10:00 P.M. Then I go home to get some rest!

What's your diet like?

I eat pretty well. But I have a major sweet tooth. I eat lots of green vegetables. I love broccoli. A regular meal for me would be a huge plate of broccoli, some fish, and a little rice.

© James Levin

Weightlifting can be dangerous. That's where personal trainers come in. "I make sure my clients do their exercises correctly," Kirk explains.

I try not to eat past 8:00 at night. Your body slows down in the evening. It's harder to digest food then.

What kind of music do you listen to when you work out?

It depends on what body part I'm training. Normally, I train with light music. But if I'm working out a body part that needs extra work, my music is very **intense.** Usually, that means hip-hop or hard rock.

What are the gyms in New York City like?

Things have changed a lot in the past few years. Gyms around here used to be filled with "muscle heads." Those guys just wanted to look big and throw their weight around.

These days, people come from all kinds of backgrounds. Some are bankers. Some are pro athletes. Some are waiters and waitresses. And, in New York, there are also actors, actresses, and models.

That's one of the best things about gyms. You get to meet all sorts of people there.

How has working out helped you in other areas of your life?

It has taught me to work hard. And it has taught me how to set goals and meet them. It has also given me a sense of balance in my life. Say I've had a hard day. I always look forward to my workout.

Would you want to be a personal trainer? Why or why not?

News Flash!
Myths About Steroids

Want to bulk up fast? Don't be fooled by steroids. Steroid abuse can cause serious side effects. Like what? For starters, steroids can cause acne and baldness—for men *and* women! Men can also experience shrinking testicles. And women can grow facial hair!

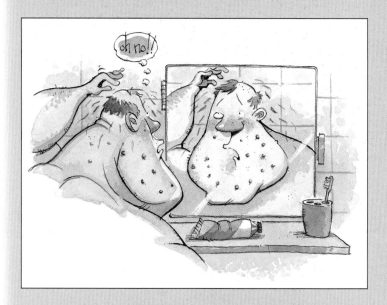

But that's not all. Steroids can make your bones stop growing. They can damage your heart. And they can even cause cancer.

So what are steroids? They're man-made versions of a male **hormone**. Steroids are sometimes used for very serious medical problems. But guess what? Small biceps *aren't* a serious medical problem.

Here are some common myths about steroids. Take a look. You'll find out you can't believe everything you hear in the locker room.

MYTH: Steroids are safe if you take them in cycles.

FACT: Some people think you're safe if you take steroids for a few weeks and then stop. That's just not true. *Anytime* you put steroids in your body, you could damage your health.

MYTH: Steroids are only dangerous when injected.

FACT: Some say that steroids are dangerous only if you inject them into your body with a needle. This is completely false. It is also dangerous to take steroids in pill form.

MYTH: It's safe for young people to take steroids for a short time.

FACT: Some young people think that nothing bad will ever happen to them. And they think that only older people get side effects from steroids. Nope! In fact, steroids are very dangerous while you're still growing.

Ring Master: Stephanie Jaramillo

*How would you feel if going to the gym meant getting punched in the face? That's what Stephanie Jaramillo faces every workout. She's one of the nation's best boxers. And her workout involves throwing and **dodging** lots of punches.*

How did you first get into boxing?

When I was young, I saw Mike Tyson training on TV. He was dancing and punching the bag. I thought it was so cool. That's what first caught my eye—the training part. So I told my parents I wanted to learn to box.

What did your parents do when you said you wanted to box?

They weren't happy! They always said no. Girls weren't really boxing then.

Finally, my dad got tired of me bugging him. He said, "I'll make you a deal. If I see girls boxing

© Kip Malone

Stephanie Jaramillo has been boxing since she was 13. She has become one of the nation's top amateur boxers.

on TV, you and I will look for a gym."

About two years later, I was watching TV with my parents. Women's boxing came on! I was so happy. I started jumping up and down. My mom was mad. My dad just started laughing. He couldn't believe it. I said, "There it is, Dad, right there on TV." Two days later, I found a gym. I've been training ever since.

Say you're spending a day training. What do you do?

Right now, I run five to six miles in the morning. Then I go to the gym to work on my boxing skills. I do three **rounds** on the heavy punching bag. Then I do three rounds on the speed bag. Then I do three rounds of **shadowboxing**. Finally, I jump rope for ten minutes.

After that, I go home to eat breakfast. Then I go to another gym. There, I lift weights and do aerobic exercise. My mother usually comes and exercises with me.

Next, I swim or run again for three or four miles. Then it's back to the gym for more boxing.

Do you ever get funny looks at the gym because you're a female boxer?

At first I did. But there are a lot of women boxing these days. It's not as unusual as it used to be. Anyway, when I'm at the gym, I have to be focused. I can't worry about what other people think.

What do you do to get ready for a fight?

A week before a fight, I take a whole day off and go to a salon. That's like a day-spa. I relax. I have a massage or a mud bath. Stuff like that. Basically, I don't think about boxing or anything else.

The next day, I wake up and have a light workout. Usually, I also have to do some interviews with TV and newspaper reporters. Then, that whole week, I work out with reporters watching.

If my fight is out of town, I usually go one or two days early. I check into my hotel and hang out. I like talking to all the other women.

Does it hurt to get hit?

I've never been knocked down. But I've

been hit pretty hard. That's just the sport. If you step into a ring, you're going to get punched. Usually, your **adrenaline** is going. So you don't really feel it.

After the fight, you feel the pain. But it's important to remember that boxing is a sport. The point is to *compete,* not to hurt people.

What do you do to stay safe?

We follow the rules used in the Olympics. Those rules are different from the rules used in professional boxing. For example, we have to wear headgear. Professional boxers don't. Also, our gloves have more padding than theirs.

Most important, Olympic rules force you to fight "outside." That means you fight from a distance. You use jabs to score points.

Professional boxing is usually "inside fighting." That's closer fighting, with punches to the body and the head. And that's how people get hurt.

What do you like best about going to the gym?

I like seeing different kinds of people

working out. There are young people, old people, people trying to build muscles, people trying to lose fat. Everybody's there.

Also, when you work out with these people, they become your friends. Going to the gym is like hanging out with friends! That's what I like most about it.

Why do you think Stephanie wanted to become a boxer?

Have a Heart

So, you're ready to work out. Don't forget the most important muscle: your heart.

Sometimes, even real gym rats don't do enough for their hearts. That's a big mistake. You need a strong heart to work out the rest of your body.

Exercise that works out your heart and lungs is called *aerobic*. When you do aerobic exercise, your heart beats faster. And you breathe harder than usual. Some examples of aerobic exercise are running, swimming, walking fast, and riding a bike.

Try to add aerobic activities to your everyday life. That way, if you don't have time to go for a run, you'll still give your heart a workout. Just 30 minutes a day can make a big difference.

Here are three ways to work out your heart every day.

1. **Ride your bike.** Driving a car can be fun. But if you ride your bike instead, you'll get some exercise. For example, riding your bike to and from school would give your heart a great workout. And it would also save you a few bucks on gas.

2. **Take activity breaks.** Are you stressed out? Mentally fried? Upset with your family? Don't turn

to the TV for comfort. Pick up a basketball or go for a swim instead.

3. **Walk more.** Take the long way to visit a friend. Walk up stairs instead of taking the elevator. Keep your body moving. (Note: Walking to the fridge or to your car doesn't count!)

The more aerobic activities you do, the healthier you will be. Plus, you'll eat less. It's easy to eat a bag of chips while you're watching the tube. But it's a lot harder when you're throwing a football!

Glossary

adrenaline *(noun)* a chemical your body makes when you're excited, scared, or angry

aerobic exercise *(noun)* activity that makes your heart and lungs stronger

biceps *(noun)* the muscles on the front of your arms between your shoulders and the inside of your elbows

caffeine *(noun)* a chemical in tea, coffee, and some soft drinks that speeds up the body

carbohydrate *(noun)* a substance in foods like bread, rice, and potatoes that gives you energy

client *(noun)* a person who uses the services of a professional; a customer

contagious *(adjective)* something that spreads easily

dodge *(verb)* to get out of the way

hormone *(noun)* a chemical that your body makes to help you grow and develop

intense *(adjective)* showing strong emotion or feeling

motivator *(noun)* someone or something that pushes you to reach your goals

nutrient *(noun)* something that your body needs to be healthy

physical therapist *(noun)* someone who helps people strengthen muscles that have been hurt

promote *(verb)* to let people know about something or someone

resistance *(noun)* a force that works against something

round *(noun)* one period of competition in boxing

saturated fat *(noun)* fat that comes from animal products like meat and dairy

shadowboxing *(noun)* boxing against an imaginary person for exercise

slalom *(noun)* a sports event in which skiers have to move back and forth between markers, called gates, as they ski down the hill

stationary *(adjective)* something that doesn't move